These Gossamer Recollections

KATHRYN KNOWLES

MAD
ENDEAVOUR

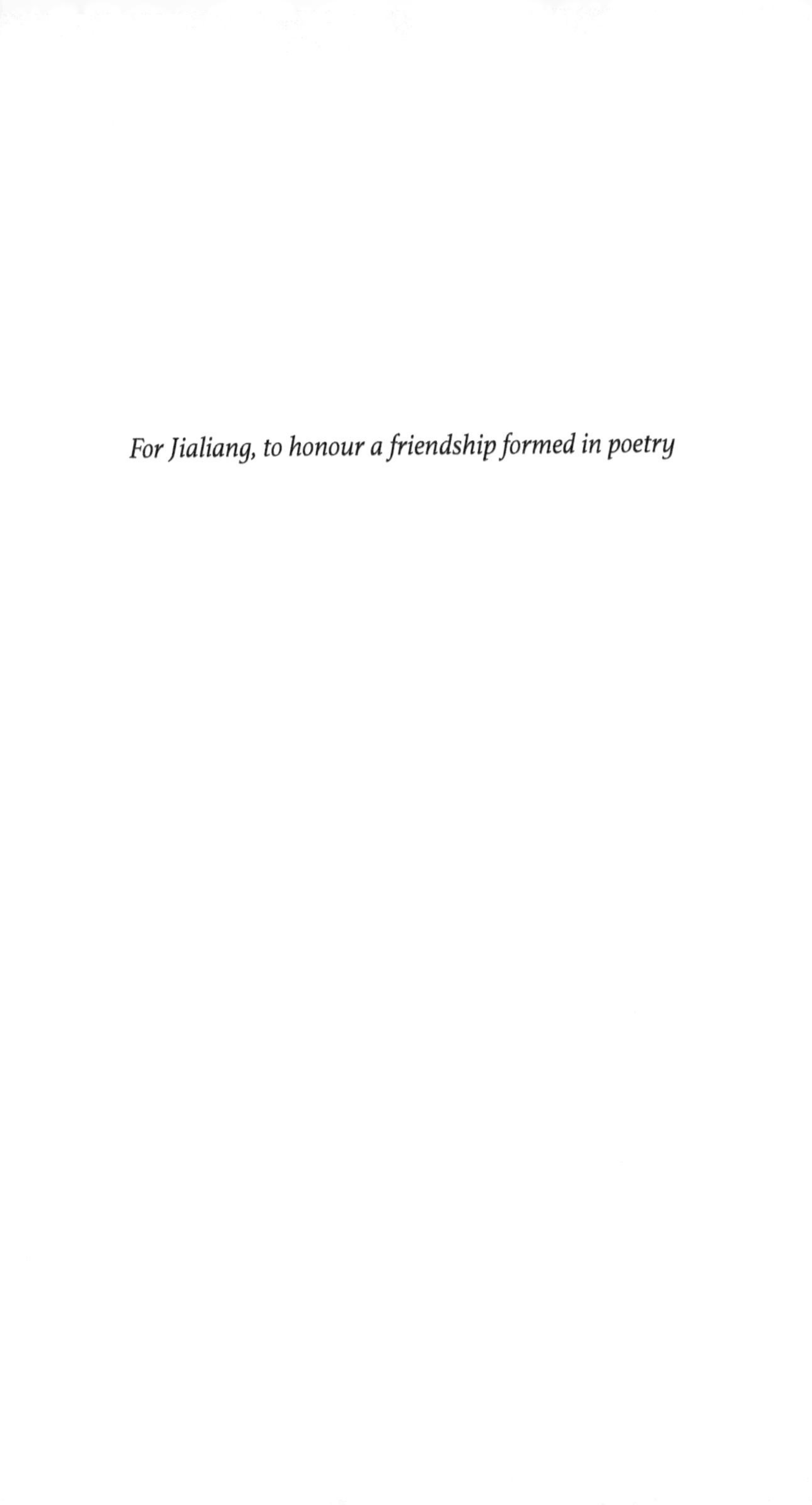

For Jialiang, to honour a friendship formed in poetry

INTRODUCTION

The following collection of poems began as a simple challenge I set for myself. The goal was to write thirty poems in thirty days, during National Poetry Month. I set myself this challenge in late 2019 and all I needed to do was wait for April to roll around. I think many people mistakenly believed this was a pandemic project, something I did to cope with the boredom during isolation in 2020. But that isn't how it began. It began as a fascination with language and a need to explore poetry more in-depth and see what happened.

I spent the month writing poems, bleeding out my anger, frustration, and loneliness onto the page. Over time, I realized that my role as a poet is to open up a vein, so to speak. To be raw and real and share my human experiences with the world. I think society needs artists to express themselves because it provides a safe space or a framework for others to do the same. We all want to feel things and experience as much as this world has to offer. But we have limited time here to do it. So, we turn to artists to share their experiences so we can glimpse some more of what it means to be alive. We can feel what they felt, see what they saw, learn what they learned.

After the success of my first National Poetry Month challenge, I did it again in 2021, 2022, and 2023. This collection of poems includes most of the poems I wrote during these four years, and a few others that fell outside the monthly challenges.

Needless to say, a lot happened in four years, so the poems cross a wide range of emotions, tones, and themes. When I sat down to compile this book, I decided the best way to do it would be to categorize them by emotion.

Each section of this book contains the poems which I feel share a common emotional thread, be it anger, surprise, disgust, fear, sadness, happiness, or some variance in between. Each new section begins with a short, stylized poem to set the tone. I call these Poetical Musings because they feel more like abstract thoughts. The overall emotional arc of the book progresses from a place of surprise and wonder, through the more turbulent arenas of anger, fear, and sadness, before breaking through to happiness at the end.

At the back of the book, I've included some notes about a few select poems, in case you're interested to learn more about the context for them. But feel free to ignore me and just find your own meaning in the words. Nothing would make me happier than knowing my poems mean something different to different people.

So, with that, I leave you to feel whatever you need to feel as you read this book. I hope my poems can help loosen some things inside your heart and give you a space to explore your own life, your own stories, your own gossamer recollections.

This life, ephemeral,
is transient beauty
born of stardust,
momentarily shining in the sky.

Whispered Memories

Our stories, etched with fading ink
On finest vellum sheaves—
Mysteries to deepen with every passing year;
Memories whispered to silent ears
Are scattered among the misplaced thoughts—
These clues and hints we scarcely understand.

Library Eye

The library in my eye is full of leather tomes that creak
their spines on opening.
The type-set words are jumbled at the iris,
Black ink tales and maps to hidden worlds,
The parchment, bleached and wrinkled, floats away
beneath new quills.
The stories mix in inky hues of yarns and characters I
used to know,

And long ago forgot.

Space to Shine

What cosmic cookbook writes prospective life?
What map will chart us out in space and dust?
The future burns too hot.
It melts the dreams of timid moonrise,
Seeping through the cracks of conscience into void.
That place of dense forgetting compresses souls to
diamond lights
That spiral out in search of space to shine.

The Girl with Cherry Blossom Hair

The girl with cherry blossom hair has
snowflakes in her eyes.
Her linen bones and mossy skin are clothed in
frozen bark,
while rainbows in her veins erupt and
scatter beams of crayon light
to blur the lines of sterile black and white.

The girl with cherry blossom hair holds
starlight in her palms.
Her diamond nails and velvet touch are strong with
sun-drenched warmth,
but windstorms in her soul exhale and
whisper sounds of conscious thought

to fill the void of what the world forgot.

The Tree Awning

The trees that grow down from the sky
Wear leaves that dangle, float, and fly;
They brush against the skin of earth,
So feather light, and full of mirth;
The roots twist patterns up so high,
With knots too tangled to untie;
The awning for the world below;
This parasol of things that grow.

Heard

Spoken—
Not sung or screamed—
Set free to softly float
From ear to ear and back again;
To hear.

Bent Horizons

The sky that folds in half
Leaves a crease upon the sun
To split the beams and cast the day
In crooked paths away,
Along these mirrored, bent horizons.

The Truth of All Truths

Here, at the genesis of human thought,
We ponder this world's greatest mysteries.
We wonder what's next; what's real and what's not—
Humans, so needy for quick guarantees...

What if the answers are not what we sought,
But only the sort to cause more unease?

Would we abandon this calling to know
The truth of all truths, begun long ago?

The Marble

The small marble rolled across the floor
And stopped short of its destination.
In the once spherical spinning glass
Are separate swirls of jade and sun.
A second marble rolls to meet it,
The faint clinking sound of glass on glass—
Not hollow like wine goblets cheering,
Nor resonant like knocked-on windows,
Just a soft sound of tapping marbles,
A click of satisfying wonder.
The indulgent joy to watch them meet,
Blending their patterns of different tints
Like captive cats' eyes, gazing at us,
Daring us to roll them all again.

The Kindness of a Thought

The kindness of a passing thought:
Wisdom at its state most pure—
To travel far and reach our hearts,
Inspiring acts that move the earth.

Wisdom at its state most pure:
A simple beauty of intent,
Inspiring acts that move the earth
And bring us closer to the sun.

A simple beauty of intent:
To travel far and reach our hearts,
And bring us closer to the sun;
The kindness of a passing thought.

The Flowerpot Hat

The flowerpot hat
plants seeds in the mind
to sprout creeping roots
that soak up thought
and bloom emotion on the face.

Seashell Shoes

With seashell shoes, we walk on air
And surf atop cloud cover waves
That whisper when the wind is fair
And whistle through dark crystal caves.
But deep below in salty graves,
The rockweed gazes through its glass
To see how skylight blue behaves
And wait for low tide's sleep to pass.

We're All Adrift in Time and Space

We're all adrift in time and space,
In orbit at the speed of light,
Like shooting stars in cosmic night
That vanish quick without a trace.
When gravity takes its embrace,
And squeezes earthlight out of sight,
We're all adrift in time and space,
In orbit at the speed of light.
The crescent moon is face-to-face
With nebulas that swirl despite
The umbra's ever-gaining height.
And, blinking out with gentle grace,
We're all adrift in time and space.

Garlands of Fireflies

Garlands of fireflies
Drape the summer skies.
With braided strings
Of burning wings,
In wreaths of twinkling lace,
Like woven, starlit grace,
These vines of light
Incite the stagnant night.

They Call You Monster

They call you monster
And fear your oddities:
Your green skin, slashed with scars;
How you strain towards the light
You crave to stay alive.
They keep you captive and contained,
Held back, restrained.
They call you monster
And misconstrue the word.
Not gross, grotesque or brutal;
Monstrous in your majesty,
Too wild to be ignored.
No villain asking to be feared,
An awesome being, born to be revered.

She Sees Through Violet Orchid Eyes

She sees through violet orchid eyes,
Beholding love and graceful strength.
Her fronds of wisdom span the length
Of vistas bathed by keen sunrise.

Her vibrance pales the bluest skies
And dares the ardent few below,
Who envy her impassioned glow,
To bloom with colours bright and bold
And grow with vigour uncontrolled;
She shows them what they yearn to know.

"It's hailing outside," said the whale

It's hailing outside,
a storm as sharp and cold as steel
or shards of mirrored glass.

The sky is smearing.
Its colours bleed and blend around
just like watercolours

that drip off the brush
to trickle down into the seas
and stick to salted whales.

The rainbow swimmers
break up through the swelling surface
to lick the painted hail.

It tastes sweet but dry,
since the sky has been fully drained
and all its colour bleached.

The blinding white sky,
imposing in its emptiness...
Just a blank canvas now.

The lies of promised time

poured out of him, scattering on the sighs

of unfulfilled hope,

like sand from a shattered hourglass.

We Eclipse the Tourmaline Sun

As we eclipse the tourmaline sun
From clear to blackened night,
With well-diminished spectrum sight,
Its lustre harkens life undone,
As we eclipse the tourmaline sun.

When smoke obscures and drowns the light,
Blurring lifeless chalky white,
The death of daylight has begun,
As we eclipse the tourmaline sun.

The hope of morning once burned bright
With ups and downs in endless rite,
But now the end of ends has won,
As we eclipse the tourmaline sun.

I Walk Rhythms on the Floor

I walk patterns on the floor,
  An art of woven limbs
  With lines and shapes
  Dictated by my whims.

I walk rhythms on the floor,
Stride songs of woven limbs,
  With tunes and shapes
  Conducted by my whims;

The dirge of heavy footfalls
Beats such existential hymns.

Mail-Order Dream

I ordered a dream in the mail,
and it came with a crack in its frame.

No refunds.

No exchanges.

All dreams are final sale.

Crystal Apple

A purple-coloured crystal ball—
In truth, an apple doomed to fall
And break future visions on present ground
That found them unpleasant.

The Storyteller

The storyteller, grey with age,
With broken pen and empty page,
She tells her tales upon the wind
And waits for echoes made
To find their way back home again
From whence they may have strayed.

The Parallel Self

Hidden in time, out of sync, out of sight,
Is the parallel self that turned right
Where I turned left and found myself here.
If we could but talk, if we could but hear
All the stories of us that exist,
And—adding it up—find there's nothing we missed,

Maybe then we would be content.

The Plant on the Bowed Windowsill

The plant on the bowed windowsill,
With its long spidery blades
And cracked terracotta urn,
Where once its roots had burst through,
Stands frozen in time,
All withered and brown,
Bent forward in exhaustion;
Too worn to reach for the sun
Or suck up the rain
Of the tearful dew,
Whose drops of perspiration
Used to shelter safely there.
But, frail, it crumbles to touch,
Adding dust to fallow dirt.

The Jigsaw Man

The jigsaw man
Is built of cardboard pieces,
Ill-fitted together to form his soul—
Whenever a piece goes missing
He takes one from another
Until every carton rattles
Its incomplete portrait
And his face becomes
An abstract patchwork quilt
Of every image he's ever borrowed,
And every other puzzle
Is left littered with empty holes.

The Sculptor

The sculptor chisels slowly
To free his art from stone;
Hours, years of endless toil,
Knelt by his granite throne.

The stone resists and struggles
To keep its blockish frame;
Rigid, cold, unyielding grey,
With surface all the same.

The sculptor, growing weary,
Feels hope begin to drain;
Broken, lost with nothing left,
Resigned to daily strain.

One wrong move, the vision cracks
And crumbles down to sand;
Meagre, mundane daily dust,
With no bright future planned.

The Brass Vase

The brass vase,
Once armed with hate,
Now waits for petal falls;
The flowers wilt and brown,
And dry against its walls.

The brass vase,
Now caked in time,
Once bright with fighting pride,
Now measures pain and loss
By all the petals cried.

The brass vase
Stands by itself
Amongst the flowers red;
Its vigil of regret
Displays the long-since dead.

The Garbage Bag Vulture

Behold the garbage bag vulture
now swooping through the skies
on gusts of hazy breath—
most unnatural as it flies.

The exhausted city coughs
and clogs the air with tangy clouds;
that humid human stench
gives rise to wings of ruin.

The soaring bird inspires awe
at first, but closer sight
betrays the wasted truth;
the omen of that fouling flight.

Dusty Promise

With shadows bleached by summer rays,
The edges smudge towards the sun;
Such pastel hues of dusty promise
Veil our filigree horizon—
The mirage of endless splendour.

Industrial Grey

The sky is raining chains
That clatter and clink
And, falling, dent the earth;
While metal trees loom and sway
In the fraught magnetic breeze,
As leaden mountains pierce the sky
And spew forth alloy sparks
That fly through chain-link webbing
And colour in the dots of life
With industrial slate grey.

Frozen Secrets

Within the gently falling snow,
A mystery dares you to know—
Whichever truth you still might seek,
The bitter wind will now bestow.

When snowflakes hit the forest creek,
It freezes truth in winter bleak.
The secrets sit with icy eyes
And wait for you to finally speak.

You shed your overcast disguise
And skate through fear that never dies.
Frost bites and chills the weathered voice
That shivers underneath the lies.

Tarnished

The tower of tarnished plastic,
With holes on its face,
Spews clouds of dust and dried-out air
To clog the sky and suffocate the wind.

Sepia stains of time;
The filth of existence;
Its body now smothered
With layers of dull neglect.

Patinas of needless permanence
Dye its heavy life.
This ugly, broken, vulgar frame
Must judge itself in never-ending death.

The Mistaken Edifice

The limestone limbs crackle and break,
And crumble to the ground.
The wooden bones tremble and shake,
And creak their wretched sound.

The plaster god who built this case
Is laughing in the sky,
While termites wrinkle up this face,
And sawdust fills this eye.

The concrete veins, heavy with ache,
Are petrified and bound.
The plaster god's greatest mistake
Ought never to be found.

In Bleeding, Winged Flight

The bloodshot tinge around the world
Is bleeding into sight;
The crimson veins now feed the trees
To rust the leaves in spite
Of any birds who need to take their flight.

The canaries tarnish quickly,
Much faster than the hawks
Who flap their oozing spectral wings
And stain the sandstone rocks
That stood to worship searing equinox.

The sanguine ink of feather quills
Can etch their tears in vines
Upon the coral tree trunk bark,
Stained red with nature's wines,
And blend, distilled, amid the tart bloodlines.

Epitaph of Family Joy

It's a shattered, broken frame
Of a blurry photograph
That sits crooked on the mantle piece
With its fake and frozen laugh.
We all ignore its sepia tone,
Its amber longing woe,
Like we're all immune to time,
Heedless of the clock bell chime.
It's the epitaph of family joy
From simple years gone by
That can only fade and die.

This **diamond** soul was forged
in tons of **pressure,**
destined to **shine,**
forbidden to break.

The Waning Clock

The ticking clock is waning,
Its hands stutter and stick,
It's desperate plea to be released—
To cease its perpetual count;
This endless tally of hours spent—
Goes unheard; misconstrued.
Instead, they come to wind it up.
They urge it to continue,
Twisting, turning its dials,
Winding till the grinding crunch
Of gears is followed by the
Hollow boom of silence.

Pastel Sheens

The world is blurry at the edges;
The wind begins to smudge the sky
Like pastels on my fingertips
That glue together blues and whites;
To fade away the vibrant light
It cakes on sheens of make-believe,
Creates a bland patina
That buries creativity
And drowns imagination.

Cyberpunk

<html>
<body>
<p>A rebel rides on waves of information,
Navigating webs of worldwide lies.
His veins of frayed and tangled fibre optics,
Wrapped in strips of patterned punched tape skin,
Must upload blasts of constant update culture
To numb his own planned obsolescence. </p>
</body>
</html>

Counting

I count the days until...
I count the weeks,
I count the months,
The years, the—
I count and count—I fear—the endless counts
Till nothing counts at all.

Tinted Wine

49

This sneaking, twisting, creeping vine
Might, tightly 'round the heart, entwine
To clench and squeeze its pounding beat,
Leach all its vibrant, living heat,
And sap its essence, use its sweet
Red blood to tint its palest wine.

To Be a Villain

What if you aren't the hero of this tale?
Perhaps your villain heart is stronger now…
It hears those hidden thoughts of hate that wail
Inside your mind, contorting, asking how
You might break loose from any solemn vow
Of love or truth, instead, to spread your lies,
Decrying all the things that you despise,
With slick persuasion, craving fear and pain;
Impassioned there, but numb to all the cries
Of those who suffer for your cruel disdain.

The Broken Sky

The broken sky is cracked in half
and bleeding poison light,
with flames that flicker at the seams
and lick the kindling clouds
till dust and desiccated grey
shade the burned-out vista.
And, hissing, dancing through the gaps,
a shattered web of orange
entraps us like a burning net
which chars and scalds the world
bestowing latent glowing embers.

Peaceful Indifference

You strained for years to reach the end of your rope,
and there, stretched taut and stymied,
you collapsed into inertia
and welcomed the peace of indifference.

The Fireplant

The fireplant, with flaming leaves
and smoky tendril vines,
has foliage to shame
the autumn trees.

Its crimson stems
and harvest fronds
may crackle brightly
in the errant breeze.

The stem, a stick of dynamite,
a candle waxed in soil,
with irate, fuming roots
that no one sees.

Not roots, but wicks
that slowly burn
beneath the blistered earth
in vengeful weaves.

They sizzle as they smoulder
into ripened, ashen strips.
Its temper chars and burns
its last degrees.

The plant ignites,
as beauty turns
to wrath to punish those
who praised it for its leaves.

To Drown in Cacophony

Confined in my head, I try to make space;
To clean out the junk and silence the noise.
That ever-grating buzz and hum,
Of the hammers and angry drills,
As someone constructs a temple, a shrine,
To the cacophonous medley of screams.
The cries for attention ring out,
But the list'ners have all gone numb—though still the
sound persists.

It grows louder and still more demanding.
In the channels of my mind, it echoes
Like battle hymns of unseen foes,
Driven by insatiable thirst—thirst that yearns to be
heard.

Drowning in noise, my mind rattles and gasps,
Stretched out and strained till it's rasping and raw.
Sounds stream in faster and faster,
Too fast for a drain to release.
All thoughts swirling 'round the dark, churning pool
Until, drenched and soaked, too heavy to float;
Dragged down by the current, they fall.
Crushed by the weight at the bottom—never to be heard
at all.

What Is the Point of Being the Light

"What is the point of being the light?" she asks,
"When darkness is so much fiercer?"
It grows bigger, vaster,
Engulfing all that was good—
"What is the point of being the light?" she asks.
"It's not strong enough to matter."
When every effort fails,
And nothing ever improves—
"What is the point of being the light?" she asks,
Just to be doused by heavy shade,
Drained to feeble dimness,
Too weak to shine or care.

Psychic Bloodshed

There's violent warfare in my head,
Hostile, angry, screeching at me,
An assault of psychic bloodshed,
Which detonates the sentient blasts
That drive mind shrapnel to imbed
In thick skull walls, and bang the war drums
In my ears that cue the widespread
Putrid smog of mental scrap debris,
That billows out to shroud the bitter dead.

An Elastic Band

The end comes in surges,
Stretching in and stretching out;
No painful rupture
Or snap of self-destructive freedom;
Just the agony of straining—
An elastic band,
Pulled taut, too long,
Loses its resilience;
Fractures spread, and there it stays,
Trapped on the cusp of death,
Glommed until something comes
To jostle it into disintegration.

Perpetual Motion

What you see as never-ending motion,
An illusion of energetic wealth;
The great deceit of our time.
As supplies are rationed
To stave off expiration,
We run the risk of madness.
"Better to run than walk," we say,
And collapse upon arrival,
Betrayed by lies of value,
Impoverished in our death as in our life.

A dauntless life ignites with

vivid majesty,

to dazzle the staid and discontent.

A Better Calling

I might leave in search of something great;
Some place or purpose higher than fate;
Some gorgeous calling so bright—ornate—
It dares, inspires me to create
A rich, fulfilling way to be myself:
Someone free from futile, joyless weight.

Craving Courage

If I could plant a seed of hope
And watch it sprout inside its pot
With roots of craving courage,
How freely would it flourish there?

Would leaves of paper dreams
Soak up the swaying sun
And dance on winds of chance,
If I could plant a seed of hope?

While fortune flowers once a year
To drink the light of promise,
I will coax the tender soil
And watch it sprout inside its pot.

Does faith need more than rain
To live in quiet splendour,
On stems of self-compassion
With roots of craving courage?

The earthy bed of fragile needs
Might sate that craven doubt
Beyond this dearth of dry despair,
How freely would it flourish there?

Counterpointed Paths

When syncopated life lines cross,
And fall in unison,
They beat a mono-rhythm clock
That slows and peters out
As minutes fade and flutter by
To tally wasted days.
It takes a punctuated wrench
To pry the lines apart,
And set them out again along
Their counterpointed paths;
In harmony but not the same.

A Smog of Freedom

A smog of freedom
fills the lungs
With heavy, calming peace
It blocks the noise,
and blacks the light
that burns at conscious thought.
Its numbing weight
and soothing hush
drown the frenzied dread
and slowly choke the bleak and barren soul.

If Life Should Tame You

If life should tame you,
claim your wild intent for bolder pleasure;
Let freedom be your death;
your liberation's sweet unveiling.
Born at the end of certainty,
and the launch of feral curiosity,
release your pre-penned destiny,
let loose your captive possibility
into the waters of expiration
and watch the seas of emptiness
run wild with anticipation.
Your liberation's sweet unveiling
let freedom be your death.
Claim your wild intent for bolder pleasure.
If life should tame you,
Let freedom be your death.

Keys Left to Rust

The key,
Crusted in rust,
Creaking, scratching the chain.
Where is the door that it fits in?
Still locked.

Foraged Truth

Most hungry, thirsty minds
Must forage thought in wild spaces,
Seeking hidden truths like berries
Hidden deep beneath deceitful bracken.

Doubt Lurks

It
Lurks
Above,
Always there
In silent judgement.
A hateful harbinger of doubt.

Indecision

Yes.
No.
Maybe—
I don't know.
Indecision wins
Against the burdened, weary brain.

Prism Harmony

The amethyst whales
sing their songs in crystal pools,
seeking connection
amidst schools of marbled fish
who refuse to harmonize.

The amethyst whales
sing their songs in crystal pools.
Their spectrum voices
echo prism harmony
amidst deep saltwater waves.

The Madcap Man

The madcap man makes his frantic bid
To abscond with his stolen prize,
Feeling the rush of success;
Flouting rules for the thrill
Of feeling alive,
To prove he stands
Unrestrained,
Apart;
Free.

Night of Flight

I feel the vacuum pulling me.
I hear the white noise speak
Through dim and weary sight.
It promises me flight—
No friction, no resistance—
Just endless soaring night:
Night of stars and black;
Night of time and hope;
Night of endless soaring flight.

A Fiddlehead

A fiddlehead is all curled up
Beneath the bracken canopy.
The air is damp and smells of spring
Beside the trickling riverbank.

Beneath the bracken canopy,
The fiddlehead aspires to grow
And spread its leaves across the sky.

The air is damp and smells of spring
That promises tomorrow's rain
Will glisten brighter than today.

Beside the trickling riverbank,
A fiddlehead can hold its ground
Or take the risk of running wild.

Beyond the Black Horizon's Crease

In darkness, there is restful peace,
Beyond the black horizon's crease.
For when the sun has set below,
That sombre wind can start to blow,
Unburdened by the cloaks of day,
That, at the seams, begin to fray.
Regardless of the stars or moon,
The onyx eyes seek evening's noon;
A place where flows the heavy shade
And all the light of times that fade.
Within the teaming void obscure,
We find the soul's eternal cure;
A silence at the world's repose
As doors and windows start to close.
Aloft! A skylight's great black hole,
As densely packed as leaded coal.
A quiet shroud of quilted calm
Shall coat it all in soothing balm.
A stillness trimmed with early frost
Returns the quiet winter's lost.
The frozen clouds obstruct the sky,
No rain or snow can meet the eye.
The patient, ever-lasting still
Is unaware of earthly chill,
Tranquil in this deprivation,
Sparking lights of new creation.
As silence can the sounds best hear,
So darkness sees the light most clear.

The sun is tilting west now,
the sky **ignites** with flames
of *desperate*, waning awe.

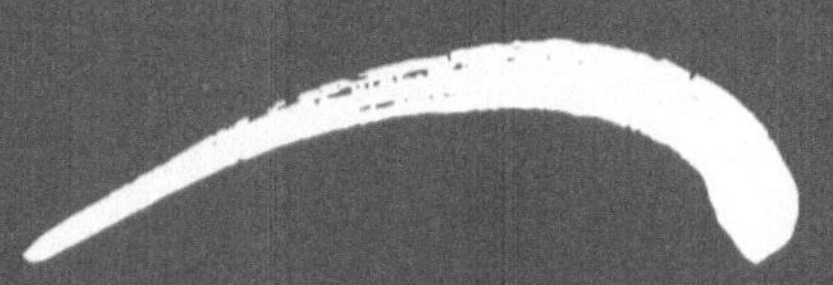

A Strange and Preposterous Affair

It is a strange and preposterous thing,
this change I'm living.
At times it creeps and crawls, consuming
me in increments; it re-invents
and then, by leaps and bounds, it lurches,
hurling, twirling, whirling me into the chaos of growth
unbidden.
I grasp at safe familiarity with routine fear,
dazed by the shades of a future I can't yet perceive.
It is a strange and preposterous thing,
to consciously supplant myself
and bask in the confounding turmoil of not knowing—
the chaos of unknowing.
The uncanny duality of growth and loss
distorts reality, threatening to end as it begins—
or begin as it ends—
and swirl, forever tangled,
as I dare to reimagine my identity.

Runaway Day

Why must the day run away,
And taunt my plans to follow,
Or halt it—hold it in my arms—
And claim it as my own?

The Juggler

The juggler awes and dazzles with his skill
While tossing stress and angst between his hands.
Wrapped up in coloured plastic, no one knows
The weight he tosses up to catch again.
Once in the air, a momentary breath
Might pass his lungs to sooth the aching dread
Of knowing one day soon he'll let them fall.

The Edge of Change

Living on the edge of change—
The precipice of progress—
Waiting for their transformation;
Forces, poised to linger.
Hostile in our impotence,
Impatient in our stagnancy,
On edge and strained, we chafe against
The bridle of suspended time,
In constant search of power,
Which exists beyond control.

Alchemical Train

A train that glides upon a golden track
Spreads alchemy in steam to mix among
The clotting layers of smoke and metal plaque,
Which stain and clog the priceless ingot lung,
And mutate age to replicate the young.
The copper-plated train now seals its door,
While mystic iron snakes across the floor.
The quickened silver casts a spidery net,
And weaves a harbinger of metal ore,
But travellers ignore the soldered threat.

A River of Lava

On the bank of a river of lava,
A man stands anchored, awaiting a ship.
Staring down at his charred black reflection,
He shivers under his dry kindled cloak.

He pops up his collar against the wind,
Cringes nervously back from the waves that
Follow the burnt-orange and crimson current
As it courses thickly downstream from him.

His skin is seared at the edges and split;
Cracked fissures erupt, spewing streams of flame;
The shrivelled tears in his eyes turn to dust,
Crusted and dried as they tarnish his face.

The flood turns to ash, the veins start to clot;
The charcoal man and his ship never sail.

The Blue Castle on the Hill

Fog drifts past the blue castle on the hill,
Framing it in the shadow of the night.
An ice sculpture in the late winter chill,
Daunting and still, its ethereal light
Shimmers through mist, always blindingly bright,
As it casts its spell on all who pass by,
Leaving its sapphire glint in their eye
And stealing away all their unused time,
To hoard it, concealed by the frozen sky,
And stand forever, a remnant sublime.

In Apartment 4D

In a shabby rental building's
Corner apartment 4D,
Beneath the loosened parquet floor,
Lurks a patient, waiting ghost:
The spirit of a tenant past.
Trapped and awaiting his chance,
He lies there watching, listening,
Biding his time till he's free
To paint the walls a deathly grey
And scratch swearwords through the air.
His anger will leach through the walls,
Perverting the other rooms;
The moans and cries of his doomed soul
Echoing through the hallways,
Terrifying all the living,
Driving them out of their homes;
The foundation will crack apart;
The windows and floors will stain;
The building will stand forever,
A vacuum of ancient lives
All drawn by the tragic imprint
Of eras and bygone times
That have no more place in the world
Or its teaming city streets.
They'll linger and dwell for all time,
Entombed in apartment 4D.

Lobster Lake

In lobster lake, the algae blooms its crunchy carapace.
Beneath that hardened aril case,
Squirm tendril water limbs.
They creep between the cracks of earthy crust
To douse the lava core
That might have warmed that cold, abrasive shell.

The Phoenix

Within a mound of ashes on the floor,
A bird is brought to life in flame and fire.
His plumes will be a swirl of crimson gold
As he's reborn from his funeral pyre.

Returning, fully-grown, towards the sky,
He'll scorch the path of winged creatures.
His sunset-streaked and unique wings will glide
Through autumn air like burning features
That shame the pallid colours of the leaves,
And blind the densest darkness with their light.
The phoenix, in his lone eternal life,
Is dying to live, stuck in bonded flight.

The last of his kind, the bird sings sorrow
That strikes the hollow chord of lonely pain
In the hearts of anyone who hears it,
Longing to hear him sing of joy again.

But his solitude is dyed in beauty
That portrays, most deeply, all emotion
Ever tested by a human's fragile heart,
Which, until now, has had no notion
What it should feel, nor how it could lose
Enough to one day forget how to feel.
But the phoenix will always remember
How to lose it all—yet still... how to heal.

So he soars above us in scenic prayer,
To share his poignant wisdom; his brave love
Can light the flame of rebirth in the souls
Of us down here, who watch him up above.

The Wry Mirror Floor

We're standing upon the wry mirror floor;
the slanted reflections are glossy, taut,
and we look nothing like we did before.
We slip through the tiles and find ourselves caught
in comparison with our effigies.
The slanted reflections are glossy, taut;
with their scrambled bones and deceitful ease,
they smile like they hold some hidden truth,
in comparison with our effigies.
Their eyes are locked in endless waxen youth;
we try not to look, we must turn away;
they smile like they hold some hidden truth.
We have no other choice but to obey
the mirror rules as we give up our place.
We try not to look, we must turn away;
avoid the sight of our likeness's face.
We're standing upon the wry mirror floor;
the mirror rules as we give up our place,
and we look nothing like we did before.

I Dare Not Dream to Go that Way

I dare not dream to go that way,
Through winding paths of loss and pain;
Run, take flight, though I must stay.

What lies beyond, I could not say,
But rather new, than this again;
I dare not dream to go that way.

So brave the next, and come what may;
You'll fight till all your fears are slain;
Run, take flight, though I must stay.

And do not stop till break of day,
When lightning clears the pounding rain;
I dare not dream to go that way.

When bonds, restraining, start to fray,
Cast off the fear that must remain;
Run, take flight, though I must stay.

And as the darkness fades to grey,
In safety there, let freedom reign;
I dare not dream to go that way;
Run, take flight, though I must stay.

Subsumed into darkness,
I cannot *yearn for light* and
risk destroying all that I am —
                    all that remains.

Granite Bookmarks

97

What granite bookmarks
count the pages spent
of universal life?
What rows of solemn rocks
can indicate the length
of chapters read?

And carved in stone,
the typeset lines
tell tales of dying dead...
whose final plotlines
hold no weight
in empty afterlife.

Ocean Sky

The clouds that move in waves,
They break upon the horizon
To crest in shallow daylight.
Low tide's sunrise streaks the fog of night—
That raven nebula's smudging gloom
Ripples and swells in aimless flow,
As the undertow of twilight
Erodes the light of day,
Draining all the ocean from the sky.

Camera Flash

A lightning bolt blinds the sky
In a cosmic camera flash
To immortalize the snapshot world
And print its living negative.
The archived memory
Of ancient sepia
Develops on plastic spools of film
That splice an animated timeline,
Where hidden figures
Sit still in portrait frowns
As they start to smudge;
The colours fog and bleed out life,
And the world is turned to black and grey,
Captured in predestined fade.

The Lightless Lamp

The lightless lamp fades into dark,
Awaiting some external spark
To burn with purpose bright and new,
Restoring its enlightened view.

In time, the blackout grows more dense
With mindless shades devoid of sense,
Like swarming fogs of murky glue,
Concealing its enlightened view.

The dimming lamp will choose to be
Consumed by its obscurity.
It will, with nothing left to do,
Extinguish its enlightened view.

The Bumblebee

The bumblebee is losing its stripes,
Its brilliant bands of yellow and black
Paled by each new flower's draw;
Rose petals bud & bloom their
Pollinated life,
Whose borrowed hue
Will one day
Fade out
Too.

Rhythm of Peace

The last day's rhythm of peace
That falls before the start of sound
Pulses, slowly metronomed,
To cue the beat of discontent.
Tranquillo bow strokes
Animate as measures well-rehearsed
Flutter from the fingertips
Into the ebbing air,
And, once heard, disappear.
The audience applauds unconscious grief.

The Crooked Dresser Drawers

The crooked dresser drawers,

    a staircase of intimate things—

        the pairless socks and

cracked elastic bands

    wear their end upon their seams

        and speak of overdo farewells

as threads unweave

    to tangle up in knots...

    how strange it is to struggle with the parting.

The Youthful Stream

The youthful stream
carves its hopeful path
in the bedrock of ancient sleep.

It strains against the density
of time and stubborn weight,
impatient for the way to widen.

Not knowing where its current flows;
not knowing what the rush is all about.

The Betrothal of Dawn and Dusk

The betrothal of dawn and dusk proposes eternal
concord;
They share our world,
Perched on the cusp of light and dark,
With tilting hearts, one favours the dark, the other, light.
They come at the brink of day, the fold of night,
And, grasping, yearn to coalesce,
But, slipping, fall apart.
Engaged in the cycle of immortal promise;
The vows of aching hope;
If they could only meet, only touch—
But in that marriage, lies the end of ends,
The end of day, of night.
They know it cannot be;
These lovers, fated to yearn, forever incomplete,
Sublime in their everlasting desire.

Hoping for New Life

He
Strays
Towards
His ending,
Hoping for new life
In that land of ageless dreaming.

Gauzy Hope

Hopes
Of
Gauzy
Chiffon lace,
Vain and delicate,
Worn to veil the truth of yearning.

A Park Bench

We named a park bench after you,
And when the evening sun is low—
Your shadow's cast in twilight hue—
The old man shuffles in so slow.
His rounded shoulders slope away
As he takes his nighttime turn,
And stops upon the bench to lay
His bones upon that wooden urn.
He'll sit awhile and watch the birds
Before he'll shine the brass nameplate,
Which bears the most important words,
That long ago did seal his fate.
We named a park bench after you.
It's a lovely sitting gravestone,
But when the evening visit's through,
The old man shuffles out alone.

Heart Shoes

He wears his heart on his feet
Like shoes.
To keep pace with the beat of life,
He'll bruise
His ever-tender soul,
And choose
A love to have, a love
To lose.

Almost Overtures

The unfinished symphony of their love;
their last great work,
composed of sighs and heavy silence;
the almost overtures.

The Glacial Princess

The glacial princess wears her crown of hailstone jewels
Atop her tendrils of icicle hair;
Her snowflake eyes bite holes through walls of false heat,
As frost creeps from the edges of her skin,
Ever closer, to freeze her slowly beating heart.
She reaches out with brittle hands,
A gesture of supplication;
A need for warmth, affection,
To save her now before the chill takes hold.

A Dog-Eared Tale

A tale,
Yet unwritten,
Reaches out from the shelf
To crack its spine upon my heart
And read
The story now scribed in my soul,
Like words typed on a page
That's been dog-eared
Too much.

A Rusty Heart

A rusty heart
Stains the smooth black paint of solitude.
Its coarse skin chafes the edges of comfort,
The boundaries of ease and practice,
As sun and rain and all the salty wind of life
Scrape away the coats of fear and doubt
Lacquered overtop—
That pristine shine of trepidation.
But love, a growing blemish,
Wears its humble imperfections—
Its patient, rugged optimism—
To crack and spread and
Flake away the layers of perfect nothing,
Till scars and scrapes are all that remain.
The ragged patterns of wild everything.

This nimbus soul,

composed of stardust dew,

is radiant in its delicate strength.

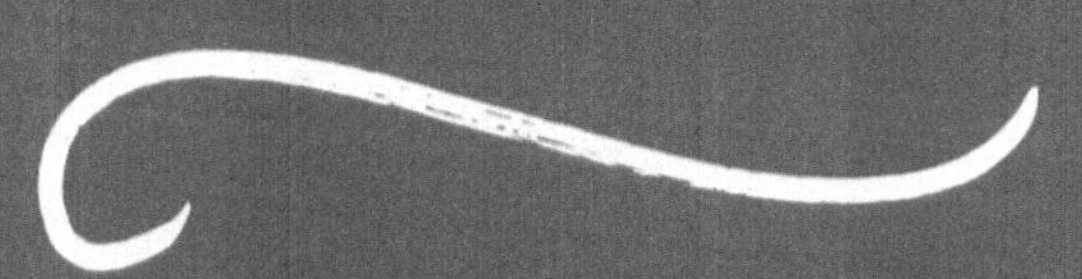

A Mad Endeavour

Sailing at the speed of light,
Streaming from the daylight quay;
A mad endeavour's shining flight.

The vessel slices through the night;
It glides across the sunset sea,
Sailing at the speed of light.

With billowed mast-clouds, grey and white—
The theatre-sky's immense marquee—
A mad endeavour's shining flight.

Untethered like a broken kite
That rises t'wards its apogee,
Sailing at the speed of light.

Ascending to an undreamt height,
With fingers crossed in private plea;
A mad endeavour's shining flight.

A soul that's strong in mind and might,
Its incandescent faith set free,
Sailing at the speed of light;
A mad endeavour's shining flight.

Our Time of Thriving

The golden green of springtime verve,
It glows in pockets here and there;
The spread of life that we observe,
Whose auric sheens speak summer fair
And streak the verdant youthful air,
Their blooms of promised, warming sun
Shall fill the soul with true welfare;
Our time of thriving has begun.

Vignette Vision

My eyes, like secret windows,
Show me private portraits of the world
With pigment palettes all my own
And patterns etched in privacy.

This vignette vision has no frames.
It sees in styles all its own.
It moves and crafts its dazzling dreams,
And draws its spotlight sketches.

It paints a picture in my eyes
To saturate emotion.
Depicting thought through living shape,
This portrait shines perception.

Starlight Eyes

The smoky starlight in your eyes,
Trails flames of cosmic fire.
It billows through galactic skies,
For all worlds to admire.

The sparkling moondust in your soul,
Illuminates the night.
It circles round the new moon's coal,
Like rims of starlit sight.

The constellation of your heart,
Is speckled 'cross the skies.
And though it shines light years apart,
I see it through your eyes.

Frosted Promise

A frozen sky reflects upon the stream,
As crystals intertwine to seal its fate
With chilly weight to freeze the warmest dreams,
And frigid cold to bite at tender hope.

A soul devoid of warmth will surely wilt...
A stream encased in ice will surely halt...

And yet, we seek a world of frosted promise
Buried somewhere deep beneath the ice.

The glacial sky is frosting on this world,
A barricade against the empty air.
It shelters us inside its vibrant peace,
Adorning us in tranquil harmony.

Awaiting us, this world of frosted promise,
Teems eternal life, beneath the ice.

Misted Dreams

When this ashen light fogs your eyes
With smog of doubt and dread,
It's not the colour of your life
Nor darkness up ahead.

It's not the grey of drowning day;
It's not the slate of endless weight.

It's the pearly sheen of early dawn
Awaiting you outside
To mist your dreams with morning dew
And light your soul inside.

Stained-Glass Vision

I watch with stained-glass vision,
Prism patterns red and blue
Tint the daily grind and toil,
Glossed in painted light to dye a hopeful hue.

In Frosted Spring

In frosted spring the buds are capped
With cotton residue.
The youthful green now cloaked in white,
And lined in icy blue,
Might start to pale and lose its life
Before the summer's due.
But in the air, a warming breeze
To thaw the cold anew.
And try and try though winter might,
Renewal still breaks through.

Petals, a Yellow Raincoat

Rainy days can drench the sunshine
As sparkled droplets of white wine
Drip from the vine, steep the earth,
And set sunflower seeds afloat.
Their petals: a yellow raincoat
That dons devoted rebirth.

In a Balloon

To glide past the mountain, in a balloon,
And float in a wide wicker crate,
Is the pleasure of late afternoon—
To glide past the mountain, in a balloon,
And loom near the orange harvest moon,
That promised it wouldn't be late
To glide past the mountain, in a balloon,
And float in a wide wicker crate.

Eggshell Dreams

With eggshell dreams and fragile hope,
we step lightly into uncertainty,
tempting fissures to entice possibility.

Behind Venetian Glass

Behind Venetian glass,
Stands a solitary rose,
Whose petals are caught in eternal wilt.
But a lonely firefly
Might one day come to shine
And share its living light to sparkle through
That crystal rose-glass vase,
Igniting sparks of colour
That have been so long missing from its vine.
It might rest upon a thorn
To drink rosewater dew,
Fermented from the years it lay in wait,
And sweetened by the syrup of the sun.

She's like a Shining Dewdrop

She's like a shining dewdrop on a fresh blossom petal—
a dome of clear potential,
glittering in the rising sunlight,
reflects our light and quenches the dawn.
These mists of fellowship envelop each new day,
each new effort,
with the comfort of faithful conviction.

She delights in our dreams and savours
the possibility of every inhaled breath;
the endless hope for the future,
and loyalty to the morning's reverie.

She's like a shining dewdrop on a fresh blossom petal—
a bead of graceful power,
sparkling with the nascent sunlight,
enchants our souls and dazzles our minds.
Our awe of amity inspires each new day,
each new hour
with the strength of friendship's affection.

We delight in her dreams and savour
the possibility of every inhaled breath;
the endless hope for the future,
and loyalty to the morning's reverie

She's like a shining dewdrop on a fresh blossom petal—
a pearl of imagination.

These **gossamer recollections**
weave to form the
abstract **tapestry** of my life.

Small Pockets

In the small pockets of the day,
We smile and laugh, share a tender,
Stolen kiss in quiet splendour,
As all our worries fade away.

In these times, we finally say
And do the things that we adore,
The things our hearts and souls yearn for;
These pockets of the day are ours
To count in minutes or in hours,
And fill with things that matter more.

We, like Zippers

We, like zippers, fold together,
Limbs joining like interlocking teeth;
A mesh of intimate ease.
We, like zippers, mould together,
Arms clasping in a knitted embrace;
A coil of warmth and comfort.
We, like zippers, hold together,
Bodies tightened in a woven braid;
A clasp of tender courtship.

The Daylight Dancer

A falling star
Eclipsed the eyes
Of the resting daylight dancer,
Who spins in time
With midday tunes
And lives in a world of sweet dreams.
With sparkling eyes,
Glittering sight,
She'll take to the sky one more time
To pirouette
Upon the wind
And choreograph the new dawn.

A Soul in Harmony

His voice like honey meets my tired ears,
So sweet and soft with wisdom as he sings
A ballad tune of hope and joy, he brings
Me comfort even after all these years.

Chordal poems with strength to transpose fears
And stand the test of time upon the King's
Most lyric songbird's rhythmic flying wings;
His soaring words can bring the world to tears.

The chorus voices share the words he wrote
To last through time and be forever ours;
To harmonize our souls like art.

So when his phrases reach their cadence note,
His melody will join among the stars
And twinkle still in tempo with my heart.

Dollhouse Town

This dollhouse town is full of figurines.
These pretty porcelain people
Stroll their souvenir streets,
With storybook lives and apple pie eyes
That shine with fairy-tale freedom
And pure idyllic ease.
This dollhouse town is flawless fantasy.

In a Shoe by the Door

In a shoe by the door,
I keep all my whims,
All my fancies and flights,
My quirks and odd thoughts,
Every strange little notion I've had.

They're squished down in the toes,
Mixed up in a mess.
With no rhythm or rhyme,
And no left or right,
Just a part of a weird passing fad.

October's Treasured Fortune

Suspended on a band of gold
The sunset sky of swirling colour
Has been wreathed in frozen stars
To charm October's fortune.

No moon nor sun could shine so bright
Nor charm the wells of inspiration
That will write our shared memoirs
And speak of treasured fortune.

Forged in the flames of affection
That burn eternally in our hearts
And will be forever ours
In lasting cherished fortune.

Suspended on a band of gold
The sunset sky of swirling colour
Has been wreathed in frozen stars
To gild immortal fortune.

My Friend

My friend, the ladybug tortoise,
Paints a pattern on its shell,
With wings to fly and own the sky,
And place to hide when over-flied;
My friend is living well.

Cherish the Years

This pleated skin on my face,
the tartan quilt of age,
bears the beauty of cherished years.

The Guardian

I've loved him almost all my life, my friend
Has been my strength though all my joy and pain,
For now and always through right to the end
Where naught but dust and stories will remain.

We are the same now after all these years;
Our half-chewed eyes on either side still shine
Within our stretched-out skin all streaked with tears
That dry forever when our arms entwine.

The guardian and keeper of my dreams;
My hopes and fears he draws into his heart
To hold them tight till, bursting at the seams,
He's old and worn but beautiful like art.

Most art we hang immobile on our wall,
But I could never part with him at all.

We Live like Sandcastles

We live like sandcastles
Built of momentary joy.
Our grains of youthful wonder,
So timeless on their own,
Bound in fleeting, fragile form,
Connect to live as one.

We live like sandcastles
Built in temporary space.
We watch the rolling tide send
Gentle waves to drench our walls
And coax our bonds apart;
Reclaim us once we're done.

In Fondness, Frozen

Those in silent reverie;
In fondness, gently frozen;
Freed by tender memory
Of passions truly chosen.

The Streets of London

I'll walk with you through the streets of London,
On a sunny summer's day.
We'll stop for delights at Fortnum and Mason,
And see shows at the Savoy and Apollo;
We'll picnic at Jubilee Park,
And listen to the musicians' drums,
As we watch jets paint flags in the sky;
I'll take you to see all the sights,
And stroll along the Thames,
Crisscrossing its web of bridges,
And listening to church bells chime;
We'll wind through the streets, patched old and new,
And travel through time and space;
Because right here, right now,
We're together again;
Walking the streets of London.

NOTES ON SELECT POEMS

I offer these poems for you to unravel and explore in whatever way is most meaningful for you. You don't need to read these notes if you prefer the mystery of the poems.

However, for certain poems, I wanted to share a bit more information and context, hoping it will deepen your enjoyment of them and enrich the experience.

"It's hailing outside," said the whale, 19

This poem has a special place in my heart. It's an odd little poem, but something about it feels very personal. In April 2020, I sat by the window, wondering what to write, and it started to hail. It was a surreal moment. Trapped in my apartment during a pandemic, watching the hail pelt against the budding trees and grass below. I think I was craving some magic, some hope—something unexpected and wonderful.

The Brass Vase, 32

This is the story of a large vase, constructed from a World War Two artillery shell casing. It fascinates me that we can take something so dark and repurpose it into something beautiful.

The Garbage Bag Vulture, 33

One day, while I sat in my apartment searching for poems to write, something fantastical happened. An enormous beast flew past my seventh story apartment window. Was it a dragon? Or a condor? A pterodactyl? It had to be a glorious creature on some sort of noble quest, because what other colossal beast could fly so high and command the skies so well?

A garbage bag. Blowing in the wind. That's right. *A garbage bag.*

Yes, I realize it was stupid of me to think it might be a dragon. But can you imagine the incredible disappointment I felt that day? To discover my mystical creature was a putrid garbage bag being buffeted by aggressive winds. To go from endless magical possibilities to actual *garbage.*

That hit hard. So, I took out my feelings in a bitter poem, complete with themes of climate change and urban development with just a hint of fatalism.

Cyberpunk, 47

In 2022, I posted on social media inviting people to send me prompts for new poems. A friend sent me 'cyberpunk' as a prompt, which was just so intriguing. I wrote this poem in response to the prompt and had a lot of fun doing it. It is a rich area with a lot of interesting language and concepts. I will definitely come back to this for future poems. Thank you, Joseph.

To Drown in Cacophony, 54

This was the very first poem I wrote in 2020. It doesn't follow any form; it was free verse. I wrote this when I was in the throes of auditory overstimulation due to never-ending construction, hence the noise metaphors. But as I wrote it, exploring my frustration, it evolved as I understood the impotence I was experiencing. I had no power to change my situation, and the more I would complain about it to my friends, family, and coworkers, the more numb they became to my troubles. Eventually, hardship becomes expected and routine, as people lose their ability to sympathize and we lose our capacity to fight. Overall, the poem uses noise pollution to explore the sensation of being trapped, and powerless, rendered voiceless by our own over-exposure to a problem.

If Life Should Tame You, 67

This poem seemed to flow unnaturally quickly when I wrote it. I think it might be one of the most complex and intriguing poems I've written. I love the depth of meaning in it, and the variety of interpretations. There is no one correct meaning, but here are a few prompts to get you thinking.

The longer we live, the more we become accustomed to the behaviours and expectations of life, the more tamed we become. And what is the opposite of life? Death. So, death in this instance can be seen as a metaphor for the opposite of captivity: freedom.

The traditional fear we feel when contemplating

death is natural. Fear of the unknown. But what if, instead, we saw it as the opposite of mundane and expected? What if we revelled in the endless possibility of death instead of fearing it?

Perhaps there is a sexual interpretation here. The words: pleasure, feral, wild, anticipation... perhaps a "little death".

In essence, this poem is about a yearning to release what we hold captive within us, a need to experience more than what we're given. Our desire to break free from the bonds of expectation and complacency and dare to embrace something more.

Beyond the Black Horizon's Crease, 76

This is one of my favourite poems I've ever written. It began as a salute to nighttime—to the peace and quiet I experience when the city goes to sleep. But it evolved into something much more layered and complex. In particular, I enjoyed playing with imagery in this poem, and some of my favourite individual lines are in it.

A Strange and Preposterous Affair, 81

This poem is a companion to the piece I composed for the Hamilton Philharmonic Orchestra. The poem and the orchestra piece are a tribute to the great, and sometimes difficult, changes we experience in life. It is inspired by my experience grappling with personal change and feeling my identity evolve into something new. Writing this poem and the music gave me space to embrace and celebrate the confusion and chaos of the process, recognizing the conflicting absurdity and triumph of life's little evolutions. Change is not about becoming something new at the expense of what came before; it is about the moment where the past and the future meet and begin to blend. Change is absurd and uncomfortable. It can be unexpected and overwhelming, but it can also be exciting, fulfilling, and ultimately so worthwhile.

In Apartment 4D, 88

I wanted to write something ghoulish and spooky. I secretly love creepy, nasty little poems where you get to play around with morbid ideas and harsh-sounding words. This poem ended up being more ghostly and unsettling than ghoulish, but I still enjoyed the horror in it. I think I would enjoy writing Halloween themed poems one day.

I Dare Not Dream to Go that Way, 93

This is one of my favourite poetic forms: a villanelle. I love the rhyme structure and the repeating refrains. I find it particularly satisfying to unlock new meanings in the refrains as they repeat in different contexts. It feels sort of like a puzzle. I have to challenge my mind to put the pieces back together and make a new picture.

Doubt Lurks & Indecision, 70-71 | Hoping for New Life & Gauzy Hope, 106-107

These four poems are Fibonacci poems, another one of my favourite poem forms. It's a very simple form, following the Fibonacci sequence, but I find it a very light, easy framework to express some poetic ideas. It is also my go-to form when I'm writing poems to incorporate as part of an electronic track in a composition. I wrote one for my piece, *Dreams of Hope,* for Accordion and Electronics, and one for my piece, *A Lure of Freedom,* for Two Cellos and Electronics. In the electronic tracks, I sing the poems and recite them, and then manipulate the recordings in different ways to make an eerie soundscape. I've written dozens of Fibonacci poems, so I only included a few in this book.

A Rusty Heart, 113

This poem has come to be one of my favourites. I don't think I set out to express such authentic emotion, but it appears the poem had a mind of its own. I wrote this in 2023, after I had fallen in love and moved in with my partner, embarking on a new life with him. In the poem, I see myself reflecting on my growth and reproving the constrained way I had been before. In my heart, I have always loved the idea of *wild everything.*

A Mad Endeavour, 117

Another villanelle. This was the first villanelle I wrote. I imagine an enormous ship, sailing through outer space, with starlight in its sails. The ship defies all odds, accomplishing endlessly spectacular feats.

It's interesting, as I was writing this poem, I didn't realize how personal it was. But the more I read it now, the more I understand I was telling myself something with it.

You may know that this poem inspired my company name, Mad Endeavour. Well, I feel like this poem is a mantra for me, a promise to keep striving for impossible, spectacular things. Sometimes I feel like everything I do is a little mad. I've always got a dozen new projects on the go, and there are so many exciting experiences I want to have. I need to be brave and a little wild. That's who I am, who I want to be, and who I need to be. This poem reminds me of that.

Frosted Promise, 121

This was my first official poetry commission. The new music collective, Slow Rise Music, commissioned my partner to compose a new piece for voice and electronics, and they commissioned me to write the poem he used as text for the vocal piece. It was the first time I wrote a poem specifically for someone else to use and attempted to convey the ideas and messages he asked me to express. He wanted a poem that expressed the concept of finding light in the dark—finding hope despite pain.

Misted Dreams, 122

This is a poem I wrote for my friend Rebecca. We all have times when we despair a little or we get overwhelmed by negative thoughts. I wanted a poem that embodied the eternal faith and loyalty of friendship. A good friend is always there to give perspective and nudge us forward. Someone who believes in us and helps us keep going—to see the beauty through the fog.

She's Like a Shining Dewdrop, 129

This is a poem I wrote for my friend Jialiang. I may have dedicated the entire book to her, but she needs a poem of her own. This poem aims to capture the essence of her friendship—the care and consideration she brings to those around her. It also aims to reflect some of her raw creative potential. An insightful and expressive musician, Jialiang adds beauty to the world in every space she occupies.

Small Pockets, 133

It has always been difficult for me to be emotionally exposed, especially regarding my romantic life. But I've been pushing myself to share more of this in my poetry. I wrote this poem for my partner, Massimo. It was the first time I'd attempted to write a romantic poem. I wanted to express the importance of the small moments, the quiet hours of the day where we spend time together and simply share our love, without stress or complications interfering. I need to remind myself to celebrate these small moments as much as possible.

A Soul in Harmony, 136

A poem to honour the poet who matters most to me. This is a poem about a songwriter; someone whose music and lyrics have been a constant balm on my soul for over half my life. His songs mean something to me I can't really explain. My friends tease me about my "obsession" with him. But I'm not obsessed with the man who makes the art, I'm obsessed with the art. The best way I can explain it is that his music is a safe space for me. It comforts, heals, energizes, and inspires me. His songs get me through difficult times and celebrate the good times with me too. I want to write poems that resonate the way his do for me. I want to write music that feels the way his music feels for me. His songs make me feel alive.

The Guardian, 142

I tried my hand at a couple of different sonnets. I was also trying to challenge myself to dig deeper and be more open, more real with my poems. In the grand tradition of sonnets, I wrote about my feelings for another person. Well, perhaps *person* is a bit of a stretch. It is a poem about a teddy bear. I've had this teddy bear since I was three-ish. My grandmother and her partner bought him for me for Christmas. Now, twenty-something years later, he's become a symbol for so much—love, safety, innocence, vulnerability, growth, change... you name it. He's been there through everything. It may seem silly, but I wouldn't be who I am without that stuffed teddy bear.

The Streets of London, 145

My grandmother was the greatest person I've ever known. She had this magical ability to make me believe that everything I ever did was perfect and beautiful. She was a simple, kind woman who made the world a better place simply by being in it. And when she left the world, she did it with more grace, strength, and equanimity than I ever knew could be possible.

A year after she died, I did some travelling and ended up in London, England. My grandmother never had much opportunity to travel in her life, but she would have loved to have seen England.

I'm not a very spiritual person. I can't claim to have had any supernatural encounters in my life. But while I was travelling around London, I had this overwhelming sense that she was there with me. It was like she'd joined me on my trip and I got to take her around the city, showing her all the things she would have loved. She wasn't just there, enjoying London; she was there, loving me as I loved London for her. It was a wonderful, joyful experience. And so, while this poem might seem to be bittersweet, I assure you it isn't. My grandmother never wanted me to be sad after she was gone. She made me promise not to be. And I'll be damned if I break a promise to her. This isn't a poem about loss, it's a poem about never-ending love—on the streets of London.

ACKNOWLEDGMENTS

First, I want to thank *you*. Thank you for reading poetry. I love poetry and the descriptive power of language. I love how we can use words to communicate so much in such a small space, and how words can have different meanings for different people. It feels magical to me. And I am so honoured you chose to explore my poetry. I hope some of my poems resonate with you.

This book of poetry certainly would not be here if not for the love and support of my family and friends. The amazing people who connected with me, showing enthusiasm as I posted the poems on social media. Rebecca, who always supports me with every new creative dream I have, sharing positive feedback and encouraging me to keep going. Mom, who read and re-read every single one a million times, sending me questions and reactions, and just really got into it. Massimo, who became a new source of inspiration, one I never thought I'd have. And Jialiang, who convinced me I was a poet and sent me on a path I never realized I needed to explore. I am eternally grateful.

I wish I could thank everyone I've ever met, and every place I've ever been, but that seems excessive. So, I'll simply say that, to me, the world is endlessly inspiring. *You* are endlessly inspiring.

Thank you for being part of this with me.

ABOUT THE AUTHOR

Kathryn Knowles is a composer, cellist, conductor, and writer currently based in Toronto, Ontario. She splits her time between writing, teaching, conducting, composing, and running Mad Endeavour.

Photo Credit: Claire Bouvier Photography

In her spare time, Kathryn enjoys taking on new creative projects (i.e. filling up that "spare" time), spending time with friends and family, tending her ever-growing plant collection (obsession), and looking at pictures of puppies and dreaming of the day she can have one of her own.

Learn more at www.kathryn-knowles.com

ALSO BY KATHRYN KNOWLES

THE QUIESCENCE TRILOGY

The Relics of Illayan

The Warrior Queen

The Age of Resonance

OTHER STORIES OF MÓRCEÁ

The Last Verratrí, a Short Story Prelude

Subscribe to the Mad Endeavour Newsletter to get a free copy
of The Last Verratrí.

www.madendeavour.com